THE CHALLENGING RIDDLE BOOK FOR KIDS

FUN BRAIN-BUSTERS FOR AGES 9-12

DANIELLE HALL

Illustrated by Mary Kate McDevitt

ROCKRIDGE
PRESS

For ALT, my 42.

Interior & Cover Designer: Suzanne LaGasa
Art Producer: Janice Ackerman
Editor: Elizabeth Baird
Production Editor: Matt Burnett

Illustrations: © 2020 Mary Kate McDevitt

Author Photograph: © 2020 Natasha Vermilyea

ISBN: Print 978-1-64611-979-0 | eBook 978-1-64611-980-6

R0

ARE YOU READY TO RIDDLE?

Solving riddles is like playing a sport for your brain. It's not about whether you're naturally smart or not—it's about practice. If you want to be good at riddles, you can strengthen different riddle "muscles." That's what this book is for!

Top Riddle-Solving Tips:

* **Read the riddle carefully—is it asking you for a really obvious answer?**

* **Think about any other meanings of the main words.**

* **Look again—not all objects are what they initially appear to be!**

In this book, you'll encounter many kinds of riddles. Some will be quick puns and others will be elaborate stories. They'll test your imagination, critical-thinking abilities, and even math skills. That's right . . . mathematicians love riddles! But don't worry, you'll practice on easier riddles first to warm up.

Along the way, you'll meet characters who appear again and again. Jacinta has a lot of pets, including Shelley, the turtle. Karim is cooking for his family, but doesn't quite have the supplies he needs. And Tameka? She's always trying to fool her little brother, Walter.

You'll also get to try some classic riddles, some that have been around for thousands of years. These puzzles are so famous that they have their own names, like the Riddle of the Sphinx. Look for these (and some fun facts about their history) throughout the book.

Remember, solving riddles means thinking in different ways, and you can always get better at it. Whether you play alone or with friends and family, happy puzzling!

WALTER AND TAMEKA

MATT

JACINTA

CHAIMAA

KARIM

FRANKIE

RIDDLE WARM-UP

Riddles ask you to think in different ways. Here are some examples of types of riddles you'll see in this book.

What has two hands, but can hold nothing?

Hint: The trick to this sort of riddle is to think about all the things that have "hands." Many riddles like this one rely on anthropomorphization: giving an object human-like qualities. The way to solve them is to imagine the human traits in the riddle attributed to an object. Can you think of anything that has hands but isn't a person?

ANSWER: A clock.

How many months have 28 days?

Hint: The trick to some riddles is to take them very literally. In other words, don't overthink.

ANSWER: All of them!

What word describes a serving of ice cream, what you do to dirty cat litter, and a juicy story in the newspaper?

Hint: This kind of riddle asks you to find something that several items have in common. Often, you'll look for a word that has different meanings when applied to each item.

ANSWER: A scoop.

Imagine you wake up in a room with no doors or windows. You don't remember how you got here, and you don't have any supplies with you. How do you get out?

Hint: Some riddles rely on you to get so focused on the second part that you forget a crucial detail from the beginning. Always read carefully!

ANSWER: Stop imagining.

Use the sentence below to figure out the five-letter word hidden within it.

Before the end of the year, Ashley, please ride into Lansing.

Hint: Some riddles will ask you to figure out a certain word from a seemingly nonsensical clue. The trick here is to identify the clues that are embedded in the sentence.

ANSWER: April. The clues are "before" (indicating where to look for the answer in the individual words of the riddle) and "the end of the year," ("April is a month in the year): Ashley Please Ride Into Lansing.

Complete the following sentence: L, & T, & ___ (oh my!)

Hint: Some riddles will look like only numbers or letters. Once you figure out what they stand for, you'll know what's missing. Can you think of a well-known phrase where each word starts with the letters above?

What's the difference between a horse and a pencil?

Hint: Many riddles are based on puns or word play. When asked about how two things might be alike or different, think about words they have in common that sound alike.

My first destroys and my second tells how quickly. Don't skip me or you'll be sorry.

Hint: Another common type of riddle describes two parts of the same word. Can you think of a compound word where the first half means "destroy" and the second means "quickly"? Together they make something you should never skip!

LET'S GET RIDDLING!

Answers can be found on page 67.

1. What has many answers, but no questions?

2. What stands when it's sitting and jumps when it's walking?

3. On what side of a mug will you find the handle?

4. What song can't you sing alone?

5. Use the sentence below to figure out the four-letter word hidden within it.

   Every other letter in the riddle has a brainstorm.

6. What do you call an insect with a sore throat?

7. Tameka can make her brother Walter believe anything, but Walter is getting older and smarter. Surely Tameka can't keep fooling him, right? After thinking long and hard, Tameka has a great idea. She bets Walter five dollars that she can stay under water for five minutes without anything that would help her breathe, like a snorkel or an oxygen tank. Walter is a better swimmer than his sister, and he knows five minutes is a long time. He takes the bet, confident Tameka won't win. How does Tameka succeed?

8. Phil's dad has three sons: Huey, Dewey, and _____.

9. Use the clue to figure out the missing letter(s).

   What goes around comes around:
   M V _ M J S U N

10. Which animal sounds most like you?

11. When does ninety minus two equal nine?

sumerian Riddle

A house based on a foundation like the skies

A house one has covered with a veil like a secret box

A house set on a base like a goose

One enters it blind,

Leaves it seeing.

ANSWER: A school.

Did you know? This riddle originated in Sumer, the southern-most region of Mesopotamia (where Iraq and Kuwait are today), perhaps as early as the eighteenth century BCE. This riddle was written in cuneiform, the world's oldest surviving writing system. It was translated in 1960 by E. I. Gordon.

12. Chaimaa is in a cold, dark room. All she has is a match, a candle, and a fireplace. Which should she light first?

13. Tameka proposes another bet with Walter. She says she'll leave a room with two legs and return with six. How is she able to succeed?

14. I run but never walk. I have a mouth but don't need food. You can give me a name, but I won't answer to it.

15. What do Texas, French, and cinnamon all have in common?

16. When does April come before March?

17. In my first life, I am tree and stone. In my second life, I bring forth ideas. In my third life, I am merely dust. What am I?

18. Solid am I, whether thin or wide,
Through a window I often will slide.
Daily am I tested and tried.
I join two parts in harmony
for I am a matchmaker, you see.

WHAT AM I? FIGURE OUT WHAT THE LETTERS STAND FOR IN EACH EQUATION BELOW.

19. 88 = K on a P

20. 90 = D in a R A

21. 52 = C in a D

22. 60 = S in a M

23. 12 = S of the Z

24. 64 = S on a C B

25. 9 = J on the S C

26. 32 = D at which W F

27. 29 = D in F (in a L Y)

28. 1 W on a U

The Riddle of the Sphinx

What creature walks on four legs in the morning,
two legs at noon, and three in the evening?

ANSWER: Man.

Did you know? This riddle originates from the Ancient Greek play *Oedipus Rex* by Sophocles. In the play, the Greek goddess Hera has sent a sphinx (a mythical monster with a human head and a lion's body) to torment the city of Thebes. Oedipus must answer the sphinx's riddle correctly or be eaten alive. Spoilers: He gets the answer right. How does this riddle work? A person crawls as an infant ("the morning"), walks on two legs for most of their life ("noon"), and uses a cane to walk as they get older ("the evening").

Odin's Riddle

What is that wonder I saw outside

before the Doors of Day?

Eight feet it has and four eyes

and bears knees above its belly.

Did you know? This riddle comes from an Icelandic tale the Hervarar saga ok Heiðreks (*The Saga of Hervör and Heidrek*). In it, King Heidrek wants to execute a man named Gestumblindi. Gestumblindi makes a sacrifice to Odin and asks for help. Odin comes to Heidrek, disguised as Gestumblindi, and challenges the King to a riddle competition. This is one of the riddles he asks him.

29. One day, Tameka walks into Walter's room and challenges him with her most absurd bet yet: "Walter," she says, "I bet you I can go seven days without sleep." Walter takes the bet. How does Tameka win?

30. I can be in a field, on your foot, or in a candy dish.

31. I am a puzzle with no pieces and require a key no locksmith can make. What am I?

32. I'm as tall as any mountain, as deep as any sea.

    And though you may not think it, you are always here with me.

33. You can neither hold me nor lose me for long.

    If you think you can live without me, you're wrong.

    What am I?

34. Without this, the earth is just "eh." ➤➤

35. What's the difference between a bird and a fly?

36. One autumn afternoon, Tameka shows Walter their father's rain barrel. Tameka says to her brother, "I bet I can add something to this barrel of water to make it weigh nothing!" Walter tries to lift the barrel and can't, so he knows it's full of water. He takes the bet, not believing his sister can succeed this time. Tameka looks at the barrel, and then does something to win the bet. What does she do?

37. Sixty appear upon every face, but one shall never win in a race.

38. What's the last member of this group? Alaska, Arizona, Ohio, ____

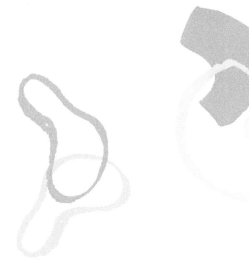

39. I have a neck, but no head,
    And two arms, but no hands.
    What am I?

40. Ten soldiers clad in white and red,
    Standing guard on a wooden plain,
    In formation by a general led,
    With one loosed strike they all are slain.
    What are they?

41. Which animals give the best hugs?

42. With behind, you'll surely lose the race. With
    down, you might skin your knee.

43. My first burns brightly, my second is a way to get from here to there. Taken together, I light up the air.

44. What you do to lights before you leave the room (1), or else you may become a pumpkin (2).

45. What king has the head of a lobster, the middle of a skink, the back of a gecko, and the tail of a scorpion?

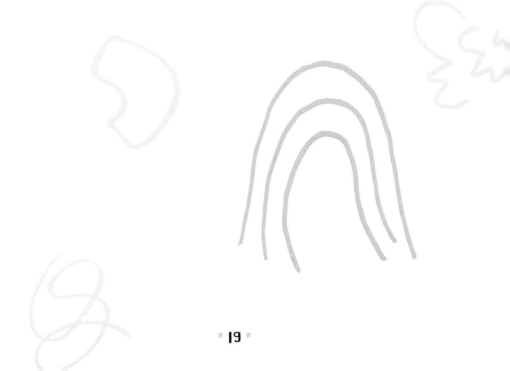

An Aztec Riddle

A little mirror in a house made of fir branches.
What is it?

ANSWER: An eye with its lashes.

Did you know? During the 1400s and 1500s, the Aztecs ruled a large area in central and southern Mexico. They were a highly educated and artistic society and valued riddles as part of learning and communication. Many of their surviving riddles have to do with subjects such as astrology, art, and agriculture. In this riddle, we can see the interpretation of eyes being a mirror.

46. How could you and a friend both stand behind each other at the same time?

47. Alex is Charlie's brother, but Charlie isn't Alex's brother. How is this possible?

48. What do doors, canals, and cars all have?

49. Think of words that have two sets of double letters, like "balloon" and "zookeeper." There are only three words in the English language. What's the third word?

50. I am in the fields and plains,
but never on the moors.
You'll find me in the mist and rain,
but never out of doors.
What am I?

51. Andre was nine on his last birthday and will turn eleven on his next birthday. How can this be?

52. Jessenia has no brothers, yet two construction workers say she's their sister. Who's lying?

53. Tameka has two red cookies and two blue cookies of the same size and shape. "I bet you that, even with my eyes closed, I can eat just one red cookie and one blue cookie," Tameka says to Walter. Walter, getting wise to her ways, agrees to her bet, but takes some precautions. He blindfolds his sister and won't let her touch the cookies. How does Tameka succeed?

54. Matt and Frankie are playing ping pong in the basement when the ball flies wide and falls down a narrow pipe. The pipe is just slightly wider than the ball, so neither Matt nor Frankie can reach in after it. How can they get the ball out?

55. Walter draws a line on a refrigerator in dry erase marker and calls Tameka in. "Here," Walter says, indicating the line. "I bet you can't make that line shorter without erasing part of it." How does Tameka manage to prove him wrong?

56. A man was washing windows on a 20-story building. One windy day, he lost his balance and fell to the ground, but he wasn't hurt. How is this possible?

57. Julio has several children. He has four sons who each have a sister. How many children does Julio have?

58. Which weighs more: a pound of cotton balls or a pound of rocks?

A Lantern Riddle

This lovely maiden eats leaves but no meat. She spins and weaves each day, with her thread transformed into beautiful clothing. Who is she?

ANSWER: A silkworm.

Did you know? In China, many celebrate the final day of the Lunar New Year with a Lantern Festival. Some of the lanterns displayed during this time are decorated with riddles. Traditionally, these riddles are "harder than fighting a tiger"! You can find a tutorial online and make one of these "lantern tigers" for your friends. Don't forget to come up with a difficult riddle!

59. What do a comb, a key, and a shark all have in common?

60. When does five plus eight equal one?

61. I must know temperature and time and I'll be fine. I have steps but not stairs and hows but not wheres. What am I?

62. Jake Spade walked into the Leadership Club meeting, where they were discussing the upcoming Valentine's Day dance. The decorations team wanted hearts everywhere. As they were digging decorations out of the storage cabinet, they found a strange box. When he opened it, Jake found something that surprised him, but made perfect sense, given the circumstances. What was in the box?

63. Name a place that has no exit, but where you can enter and escape.

64. What's the difference between a track star and her puppy?

65. Which type of tree is never alone?

66. Chaimaa is in a room with three light switches. Each light turned on by these switches contains one incandescent bulb, but they are on the other side of the closed door, and Chaimaa cannot see if they are on or off. Her mother challenges her to match each switch to the light that it turns on. Chaimaa can only open the door once, but she's allowed to flip the switches as many times as she wants. How does Chaimaa solve her mother's puzzle? ▶▶

67. I am a hothead, shortly bright and quickly dead.

68. My first is a faithful friend, my second is a forested area. Taken together, it is the North Carolina state flower.

69. What do a dog, a boat, and a town have but never use?

70. What is strong when it is unknown and weak when it is revealed?

71. Walter has finally decided to turn the tables on Tameka. He walks into the living room where she's playing video games. "Tameka, I've got a bet for you. I bet you I can write what you're thinking on this paper." Tameka sizes up her brother for a minute and agrees to the bet. How does Walter win?

Emma's Charade

My first displays the wealth and pomp of kings,

Lords of the earth! Their luxury and ease.

Another view of man, my second brings,

Behold him there, the monarch of the seas!

Did you know? This riddle comes from the novel *Emma*, published by Jane Austen in 1816. Austen wrote many popular novels satirizing marriage and romance, including *Pride and Prejudice* and *Sense and Sensibility*. She also wrote riddles! In the novel, Emma uses this riddle to make fun of a would-be suitor.

72. I am a silver road leading to a silver lake. You likely see me every day and with every slurp you take.

73. Alvaro is selling items in his neighborhood for a fundraiser. He approaches Mr. Fuentes's house and rings the doorbell. Mr. Fuentes takes a look at what Alvaro is selling.

   "How much would it be for 10?"

   "That'd be 50 cents, sir."

   "How about just one?"

   "Twenty-five cents."

   "And 106?"

   "That'd cost 75 cents," Alvaro says. Mr. Fuentes hands him the money and takes the items, not at all confused. What is Alvaro selling?

74. What flows like water, though it's completely dry?

75. You have one chair. How can you add three chairs to it while subtracting four seats?

76. Which playing card has the biggest heart?

77. When is FOUR half of FIVE?

78. I am not a giraffe, but I have a long neck.
I don't have worries, but I do have frets.
I never sing, but I have a lovely voice.
I prefer a hard shell when given a choice.
What am I?

79. What can go up a chimney while down but not up a chimney while up?

80. What word has seven letters in it, but if you remove two, you leave eight?

81. Which vegetable can a boat never carry?

82. Frankie likes oranges but not apples, cake but not cookies, pancakes but not waffles. Which does she prefer: coffee, tea, or root beer? ◄◄

83. What's the difference between a happy jug and a terrified ice cube?

84. Which bird is the best writer?

85. What goes back and forth to work?

86. I have an eye but no face.
    I am bound by time and place.
    I have a name but was not born.
    In mere days I can leave many forlorn.

87. I have six faces, but no mouth. I have 21 eyes, but cannot see. I bring loss or gain to those who throw me.

88. My first three open a door; my last five make up a floor.

The River Crossing Problem

Once upon a time a farmer went to a market and purchased a wolf, a goat, and a cabbage. On his way home, the farmer came to the bank of a river and rented a boat. When crossing the river by boat, the farmer could carry only himself and a single one of his purchases: the wolf, the goat, or the cabbage.

If left unattended together, the wolf would eat the goat, or the goat would eat the cabbage.

The farmer's challenge was to carry himself and his purchases to the far bank of the river, leaving each purchase intact. How did he do it?

Did you know? This type of puzzle was first proposed by the English scholar Alcuin (735-804). Alcuin was an adviser to the Holy Roman Emperor Charlemagne and probably wrote this collection of riddles for him. He made it seem like a collection of riddles for students, though, calling it *Propositiones ad Acuendos Juvenes* (*Problems to Sharpen the Young*).

89. The more you take, the more you leave behind. What am I?

90. Why is it so wet in England?

91. With up, it's a topic you discuss. With back, maybe you'll return an overdue library book.

92. These taught the Founding Fathers about democracy: O, O, C, S, ____

93. What can roar, hiss, snap, and devour, but has no mouth?

94. What can you put between a three and four so that the result is greater than a three, but less than a four?

95. After much thought, Walter bets Tameka that she can't cut a cake into eight pieces with just three cuts. How is she able to prove him wrong?

96. Which plant has to go to the vet?

97. What's the difference between Manx cats and a pedicurist?

98. What is clear but not see-through?
Maroon but not red?
Starched but not crisp?
Sated but not fed?

99. What do a gift, a shoe, and an archer all have in common?

100. Rearrange the letters D A I B I O N K D R F to spell a kind of bird. ⇥

101. On his 25th birthday, Florian dies of old age. How is this possible?

102. Jacinta is trying to divide some toys among her cats. When she gives each cat a toy, she has one toy too many. When she tries to give out two toys per cat, she has one cat with no toys. How many toys and cats does Jacinta have?

103. While visiting her family in Vermont, Amanda goes for a hike. She arrives at a river with no bridge. It's too wide to jump, and there are no rocks or logs available to cross on. It's also not safe to swim. Still, Amanda crosses the river without getting her feet wet. How is this possible?

104. My first is beneath you, my second moves by the inch. Taken together, I am an excellent friend in the garden.

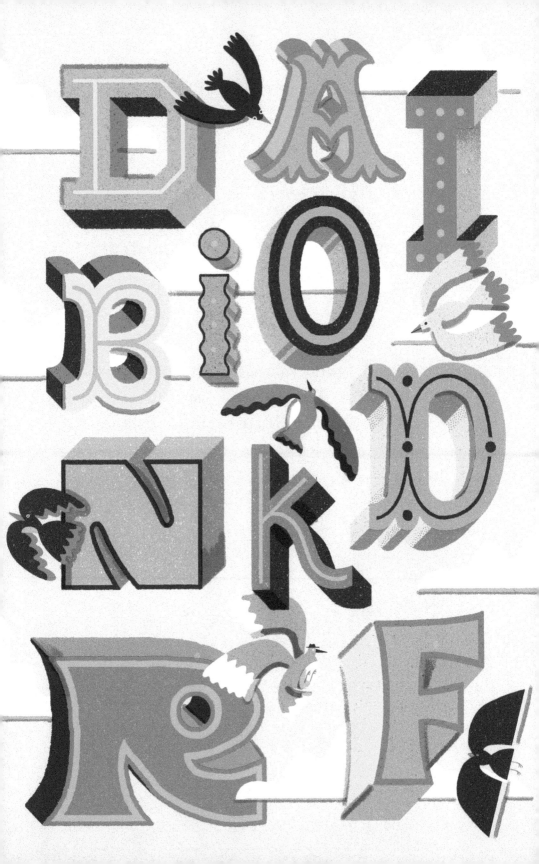

Bilbo's Riddle

Thirty white horses on a red hill,

first champ, then stamp, and then stand still.

Did you know? This riddle comes from J. R. R. Tolkien's book *The Hobbit*, published in 1937. In the book, Bilbo and Gollum engage in a riddle competition. It's interesting to see which riddles stump these characters—Bilbo knows a lot more about the "above ground" world, for example. This is a good illustration of how understanding riddles depends on what you know about the world. Not everyone is going to "get" the same riddles.

105. Your friend has chosen three playing cards at random and put them facedown in front of you. They give you the following clues: "The queen is to the left of the eight. There is a diamond to the left of a heart. There is a spade to the left of a heart. There is an ace to the left of a diamond." Perfect! Assuming all of the clues are from your perspective, you have enough information to solve the puzzle. What are the three cards in order, from the left?

106. What kind of table can you eat?

107. Tameka and Walter's mother, Vennieta, has watched her children's antics for a while, and she thinks she can win a bet of her own. Vennieta challenges them: "I'm going to go to the park down the street. When I get there, you can start riding your bikes. Whichever of you has the slowest bike will win ice cream."

Tameka and Walter look at each other, both reluctant to set off on their bikes. But, soon, they figure out a solution and then set off as quick as they can. What is it?

108. Karim's extended family is visiting to celebrate Eid, so he's making several dozen cookies. He needs to measure out four cups of flour, but he only has a five-cup measure and a three-cup measure. How can he measure out exactly four cups?

109. Use the sentence below to figure out the five-letter word hidden within it.

Initially, this color grows ryegrass everywhere elk need.

110. Use the clue to figure out the missing letter(s).

Seven new friends: G, S, B, S, D, D, and ____

111. A parent might ask you to do this to your dress clothes (1) before you can go play with your friends (2).

112. With merely some loose change, Chaimaa is able to buy something that fills a room. What is it?

113. I have an eye that never sees,
no hands, though my work requires fingers,
and a sharp wit.
What am I?

114. You have two different ropes that will each burn for half an hour. They aren't the same length, nor are they uniform in size or shape (meaning that neither rope will be halfway burned after 15 minutes). Using only these two ropes, how can you measure exactly 45 minutes?

115. Add one letter and I exist, add two, I buzz.

Remove both, and I'm still me.

116. Use the clue to figure out the missing letter(s).

These journeyed with a ring: SG, MB, PT, G, L, G, B, A, and ____

117. When Zachary is learning to drive, he leaves home for the grocery store. He's really tired and goes the wrong way down a one-way street. He even goes right through a red light! Still, he doesn't break any laws. How is this possible?

118. My first is a great source of commerce, my second is not out to sea. Taken together, I am an East and West Coast city.

119. It's been around for millions of years, but it's currently no more than a month old. What is it?

120. Jacinta decides to weigh her three turtles. It turns out that Shelley weighs twice as much as Doorstop, and Scooter weighs three times as much as Doorstop. If the combined weight of all three turtles is 30 pounds, how much does Doorstop weigh?

The Monty Hall Problem

. . . .

Suppose you're on a game show, and you're given a choice of three doors. Behind one door is a car, and behind the others are goats. You pick door No. 1. The host, who knows what's behind the doors, opens door No. 3 instead, revealing a goat. He then says to you, "Do you want to change your answer to door No. 2?"

Is it to your advantage to switch your choice?

ANSWER: If you switch, you will have a two-thirds probability of getting the car. Therefore, it is always advantageous to switch—even though you would still have a one-third chance of losing the game.

Did you know? This puzzle is named for the host of the game show *Let's Make a Deal*, Monty Hall. The reason it's better to switch is this: The only way you would lose the game after switching is if you had chosen the correct door to begin with, which you only had a one in three chance of doing. But once the host reveals a goat behind one of the doors you didn't choose, you now have twice as much information about what is behind the other two doors. Therefore, your chances of winning have doubled, from one-third to two-thirds. Those are pretty good odds!

P. S. As with any math-based puzzle that's been around for a while, experts disagree on the best strategy. Mathematicians propose and test new solutions all the time.

121. Guarded with swords,
Filled with gold,
A queen inside
with workers bold.
What am I?

122. When does a year last 687 days?

123. Achraf is washing dishes. When he looks
down, he finds more glasses in the sink than
there were before. He's alone in the house, so
how is this possible?

124. What has steps but no stairs, and if you fall,
there's only air?

125. Alone, I am heavy. Add one to me and I
become a sound. Add yet another to me
and I apologize.

126. Use the clue to figure out the missing letter(s).

An army of sixteen: K, ____, B, Kn, R, P.

127. Use the sentence below to figure out the word hidden within it.

This is the last time oxen go to town.

128. When asked if she had other pets besides cats, Jacinta replied: "Yes, my family has always had turtles, birds, and lizards. Right now, they are all turtles except three, all birds except four, and all lizards except five." How many pets (not including cats) does Jacinta have?

129. I happen in December and not in any other month. Though I'm in demand, I'm not part of a celebration.

130. You see me in water, but I never get wet.

131. This is something you use every day. The less you see, the more you've had, and to do its job, it must disappear.

132. Jacinta took one of her turtles to a pageant. Shelley came in three places ahead of the last contestant and finished two ahead of the turtle who came fifth. How many contestants were there?

133. What has legs but cannot walk, a back but cannot stand, and two arms but cannot reach?

134. My first is a direction, my second is something you do to tea. Taken together, you don't want to get caught in me.

135. When Walter gets down to the kitchen for breakfast on Tuesday, Tameka has six glasses arranged in front of her. The first three have juice in them and the last three are empty. Tameka smirks. "I bet you I can put these glasses in order, alternating full and empty, just by moving one glass." How does Tameka win this bet?

The Knights &
Knaves Problem

Two men are standing at a fork in the road. One of them always tells the truth and the other always lies, but you don't know which is which. You also know that one road leads to Death, and the other leads to Freedom. By asking one yes-or-no question, can you determine the road to Freedom?

ANSWER: Any riddle that's old enough has many variations, but the easiest way to solve this is to ask one of the men: "Would you tell me if your road leads to Freedom?" If the man who tells the truth is standing on the road to Freedom, he would say "yes." The man who always lies would have to also say "yes," because if he said "no"—that he wouldn't tell you if the road he was on led to Freedom—his answer would be true. Similarly, if either one were standing on the road to Death, he'd have to say "no."

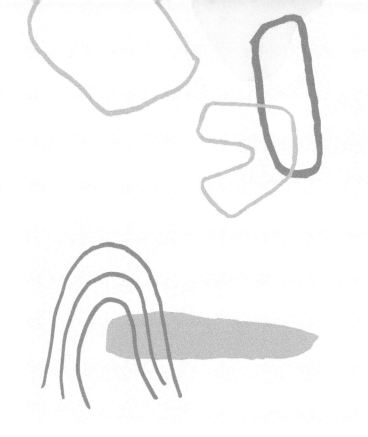

Did you know? This type of riddle has been bandied about by mathematicians for at least a century, but it was formalized by Raymond Smullyan in 1978. He named them "Knights and Knaves" puzzles (with the Knights always telling the truth and the Knaves always lying) and presented many variations. This riddle uses a type of logic known as Boolean algebra, which includes the variables of "true" and "false," much like coding. It has appeared in pop culture, including in the movie *Labyrinth* (1986) and the television show *Doctor Who*.

136. Tamara's dads have to go to work early in the morning, so she has to get herself ready for school. She puts a shoe in front of the refrigerator before she goes to bed. Why?

137. Use the clue to figure out the missing letter(s).

    Seven firm footholds: A, A, E, A, A, NA, and ____

138. I am not a cat, as my name suggests. I am not a dog, as my voice suggests.

    I am king of no jungle, preferring instead the wind and waves.

    What am I?

139. Marie buried a time capsule 50 steps away from her favorite tree many years ago. Now, even though she has the map she made then, she can't find it. Why not?

140. What flies without wings and has a tail that doesn't wag?

141. My second is a building, a shelter, a home.
My first is a tool that turns out the night,
As a whole I reach the sea and the storm,
Guiding from rocks and making dark bright.

142. You have a messy sock drawer! You have seven red socks, fifteen white socks, and eleven blue socks. If you reach in without looking, how many socks will you have to remove before you get a matched pair?

143. What is the maximum number of times you can subtract 2 from 30?

144. With on, you do it while shopping for clothes; with out, you do it to get on the basketball team.

145. Why couldn't the chicken hit a homerun?

146. I cut, grind, and sometimes shine. I am a tool that many have, but I never look the same.

147. My age in years do circles make,
I give life and never take,
Though I dance in wind and rain,
Where I stand, I must remain. ➤➤

148. Karim has his cookie dough ready to go,
but now he needs to bake his cookies for
15 minutes. All he has is an 11-minute sand
timer and a 7-minute sand timer. How can he
cook the cookies for exactly 15 minutes?

149. How do you get a magician to give you a
cupcake?

150. What has 18 legs and catches flies?

151. Which letter of the alphabet is the best
at golf?

152. Which sleeping animal destroyed the farm?

MY AGE IN YEARS DO CIRCLES MAKE,

I GIVE LIFE and NEVER TAKE

153. Ginger's friend, Pauline, calls her in a panic. "Fluffy just got out, and I'm running late for work. I'm sure she escaped to the park. Could you please go find her?" When Ginger arrives at the park, she sees four dogs. Even though she's never seen Fluffy before, she correctly identifies her. How is this possible?

154. Use the clue to figure out the missing letter(s).

    These teach us to sing. D ___ M F S L T D

155. Use the sentence below to figure out the five-letter word hidden within it.

    In the middle of the day, Peter washed your shirts, Dustin.

156. What do the words "split," "dead," and "week" have in common?

The Riddler's Riddle

. . . .

The eight of us go forth, not back,

to protect our king from a foe's attack.

ANSWER: Chess pawns.

Did you know? This is one of the riddles posed by Edward Nygma, a.k.a. The Riddler, in the movie *Batman Forever* (1995). The Riddler is a villain who always marks his crimes with riddles.

157. I am a child of dark and light,
Dwelling where the beams are bright.
But if the light should fall too near,
Swift, away! I disappear.
What am I?

158. I craft many words, but I am silent. I create
many drawings, but lack artistic skill. I can't
lift a feather, but some say I'm the mightiest of
all. What am I?

159. Use the clue to figure out the missing letter(s).

*What's missing in this series? ST, ____, RD,
TH, TH*

160. What flies without wings?

161. Frankie is an American citizen who doesn't like to travel. She lives in Hawaii and doesn't have a passport. But last week, she visited five different countries! How is that possible?

162. Use the clue to figure out the missing letter(s).

    What makes sense? P, ____ , D, Q, HD

163. With away, you discard it. With up, it's something you never want to do at school.

164. My first is a stronghold, my second has not a day to its name. Taken together, I'm a popular game.

165. Use the clue to figure out the missing letter(s).

These could not find their way home: H & ____

166. If you speak my name, you destroy me. ➤➤

167. Use the sentence below to figure out the four-letter word hidden within it.

At last, could Pedro bring his animals?

168. I am a span of time you can always see through. I am also the timepiece with the most pieces.

169. Use the clue to figure out the missing letter(s).

Twelve parts make a whole: J F M A M J J A S ____

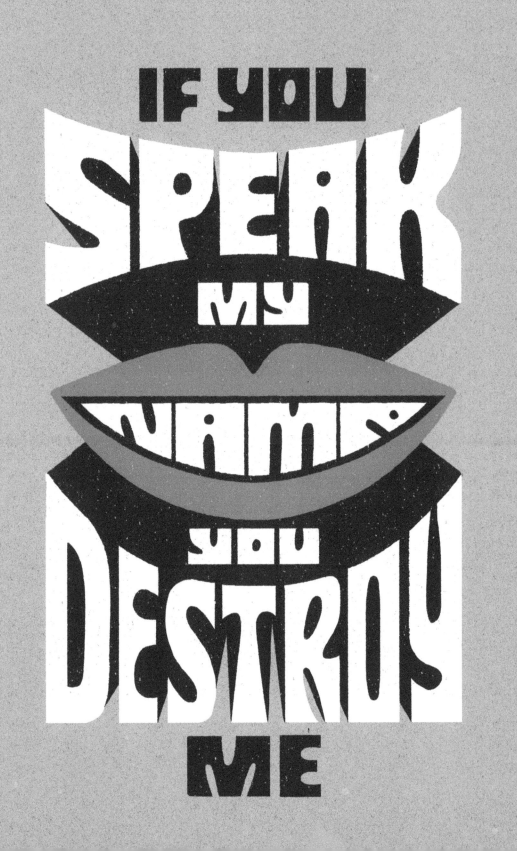

170. What is brown and has a head and tail, but no legs?

171. What's the difference between a fake dollar bill and an angry rabbit?

172. These bright artists stand in a row,
Their heads at the top and their feet down below.

One makes a dog and one makes a flower,
And if it gets too hot, they won't last an hour!

What are they?

173. What kind of cup doesn't hold water?

174. Why did Aladdin never have to vacuum?

175. Many fear me, some cheer me. I bite and fly or swing and miss. What am I?

MATCHSTICK PUZZLES

Answers can be found on page 79.

IF YOU LIKE RIDDLES, YOU MAY ALSO LIKE THESE
PUZZLES. THEY REQUIRE A DIFFERENT KIND OF
THINKING. CAN YOU MOVE THE MATCHES TO
SOLVE THEM? DRAW YOUR ANSWER IN THE SPACE
PROVIDED.

1.   Move three matches to make three squares.

2. Move two matches to make seven squares.

3. Remove four matches to make seven squares.

ANSWER KEY

1. An encyclopedia (or Wikipedia). An encyclopedia is full of information, but you have to ask your own questions!

2. A kangaroo.

3. The outside!

4. A duet.

5. Idea. Your hints are "every other letter" and "a brainstorm": r**Id**D**l**E h**A**s = idea.

6. A hoarse fly.

7. Tameka fills a glass with water and holds it over her head for five minutes. She's successfully "under water" for five minutes.

8. Phil.

9. E for Earth. These are the planets orbiting our sun.

10. Ewe.

11. When you remove the letters "ty"!

12. The match! She can't light the candle or the fireplace without first lighting the match.

13. She comes back carrying a chair!

14. River. When we talk about a river flowing, we say it "runs." The place where the river meets the sea is called the "mouth." Lastly, we give rivers names, but we don't expect them to come when we call.

15. Toast.

16. In the dictionary! The letter *A* comes before the letter *M*.

17. A pencil. A pencil is made of wood (tree) and graphite (stone). It helps us write ideas. Graphite, wood, and rubber (from the eraser) all turn to dust as the pencil is used.

18. A button.

19. 88 Keys on a Piano.

20. 90 Degrees in a Right Angle.

21. 52 Cards in a Deck (without jokers).

22. 60 Seconds in a Minute.

23. 12 Signs of the Zodiac.

24. 64 Squares on a Chess Board.

25. 9 Justices on the Supreme Court.

26. 32 Degrees at which Water Freezes.

27. 29 Days in February (in a Leap Year).

28. 1 Wheel on a Unicycle.

29. She only sleeps at night. Walter has been fooled again, alas.

30. Corn. Corn grows in a field. It's also a type of blister on a foot. Lastly, candy corn is a fall treat!

31. A secret code. A code requires a "key" to be broken. The key would be something like "A = M" and not a physical key, like we imagine when thinking of a locksmith.

32. Earth. The planet Earth includes all of the mountains and oceans. Even if you're on an airplane, you're still in Earth's atmosphere. Unless you're an astronaut, of course!

33. Your breath.

34. Art.

35. A bird can fly, but a fly can't bird.

36. She adds a hole in the barrel, draining it of water.

37. A second. There are 60 second marks on watch faces, and the one who comes in second never wins!

38. Alabama. These are all states that begin and end with the same letter.

39. A shirt. A shirt has a neck (collar) and two arms (sleeves).

40. Bowling pins. Bowling pins are traditionally white with a red ring. They stand in a triangle formation with one pin in front. A "strike" refers to knocking down all ten pins.

41. ARMadillos!

42. Fall. To "fall behind" is to lose speed compared to someone else. And of course, you don't want to "fall down."

43. Firefly.

44. Turn off/turn into.

45. Lion. This is all about letters. The head of a lobster is an *L*, the middle of a skink is an *I*, the back of a gecko is an *O*, and the tail of a scorpion is an *N*.

46. Stand with your backs to each other.

47. Charlie is a girl!

48. Locks. In a canal, a "lock" is a section in which operators can raise or lower the water level, allowing a boat to move between bodies of water with two different elevations.

49. Language. There are only three words in "the English language."

50. The letter *I*. This one is literal—the letter *I* is not in moors, doors, and more but is in plains, fields, mist, and rain.

51. Today is Andre's 10th birthday.

52. None of them—the construction workers are women. This riddle makes you think twice about who can be a construction worker. Some riddles rely on your assumptions of gender roles in order to trip you up. Tricky, tricky!

53. Tameka has Walter cut each cookie in half. As he does so, she eats one half of each cookie (and graciously lets Walter eat the other half). After Walter shares all four cookies, Tameka will have eaten a total of one red cookie (two halves) and one blue cookie (two halves). Drat! Walter's been bested again!

54. They can fill the pipe with water. The ping pong ball will float, and they can grab it.

55. Tameka draws another, longer line above it. This makes Walter's line shorter by comparison.

56. He was washing windows on the first floor.

57. Five. All four sons have the same sister. Therefore, they each have a sister.

58. Neither—they both weigh one pound!

59. They all have teeth!

60. On a clock! If it is five o'clock and you add eight hours, it will be one o'clock.

61. A recipe.

62. A diamond. In this story, you'll find the other three suits in a standard deck of cards: spades, clubs, and hearts.

63. A keyboard.

64. One laces up her shoes and one chews up her laces!

65. A PAIR-tree. (Pear/pair).

66. Chaimaa flips the first switch and leaves it on for 10 minutes. Then, she turns the light off and flips a second switch. When she walks into the other room, she touches the three light bulbs. The one that is off and cold belongs to the switch Chaimaa didn't touch. The

one that is hot belongs to the switch Chaimaa left on for 10 minutes, and the one that is on belongs to the second switch.

67. A match.

68. Dogwood.

69. A name.

70. The answer to a riddle. ("A password" would be another acceptable answer here.)

71. He writes "what you're thinking." Very clever, Walter!

72. A spoon.

73. Alvaro is selling stickers with single digits on them, like you would see on mailboxes. Each sticker is 25 cents. Therefore, the number 1 would cost 25 cents, the number 10 would cost 50 cents, and the number 106 would cost 75 cents.

74. Sand.

75. Stack them.

76. The ace of hearts. On a standard playing card deck, most hearts cards have several small hearts matching the number of the card. Since aces only have one, it takes up a larger space on the card and is therefore the biggest.

77. When you consider the Roman numerals IV (which is how you write the number four) to be two of the letters in FIVE.

78. A guitar. The long part of a guitar is called a neck, and the divided sections on the neck are called "frets." The word "fret" also means "worry." Lastly, the "hard shell" here refers to a carrying case.

79. An umbrella. When an umbrella is open, or "up," it won't fit up a chimney.

80. Freight. This word literally has the word "eight" in it once you remove the "fr" from the beginning.

81. A leek! This is a play on the words "leek" and "leak."

82. Tea. Frankie doesn't like food containing double letters, so she doesn't like "coffee" or "root beer."

83. One is filled with cheer and the other is chilled with fear.

84. A PENguin.

85. A saw.

86. A hurricane.

87. A die. A die (the singular of "dice") has six sides and 21 dots total. When you throw a die, you can either win or lose.

88. Keyboard. A key opens a door, and wood floors are made of boards.

89. Footsteps.

90. Because of all of the kings and queens who have reigned (rained) there!

91. Bring. You "bring up" a topic you want to talk about. You "bring back" something you borrowed (hopefully).

92. M for Mohawk. The Founding Fathers learned about democracy and the Law of Peace from the Iroquois Confederacy, composed of the Oneida, Onondaga, Cayuga, Seneca, and Mohawk nations.

93. A fire.

94. A decimal. 3.4 is greater than 3, but less than 4.

95. Tameka divides the cake into four equal slices with two cuts along the top in the shape of a cross. Then, she cuts the whole cake in half from the side, making eight pieces.

96. A CAT-tail!

97. The first have no tails and the second works with toenails.

98. The letter A. A can be found in all of the first words, but not their synonyms. "Sated" means

"full or satisfied," as you would feel after a good meal.

99. A bow.

100. "A kind of bird." This kind of riddle requires you to take it literally!

101. He was born on February 29th. February has 29 days only in leap years, which occur once every four years. A 25th birthday would actually make Florian 100 years old!

102. Four toys and three cats.

103. The river is frozen.

104. An earthworm.

105. Ace of spades, queen of diamonds, and eight of hearts.

Start here: "There is a diamond to the left of a heart. There is a spade to the left of a heart." This identifies your three suits and tells you that "left of" doesn't necessarily mean directly next to. You can lock in the heart as the card farthest to your right. After that, "There is an ace to the left of a diamond" means that the diamond cannot be the card in the farthest left slot. Your suits are spades (which we know is the ace from the last clue), diamonds, and hearts. Lastly, the first clue says that "The queen is to the left of the eight," which tells us that the queen must be the diamond and the eight must be the heart.

106. A vegetable.

107. Tameka and Walter switch bikes. Then, they race to the park. If Tameka wins on Walter's bike, that will mean her bike is the slowest and she'll get ice cream. If Walter wins on Tameka's bike, he'll get ice cream.

108. Karim needs to fill the
three-cup measure and
pour it into the five-cup
measure. Then, he should
fill the three-cup measure
again and pour as much as
he can into the five-cup
measure. This leaves him
with five cups of flour
in the five-cup measure
and one cup of flour in
the three-cup measure.
Next, Karim should dump
the five cups of flour back
into the canister. He will
now have one cup of flour
in the three-cup measure
and an empty five-cup
measure. He should pour
the one cup of flour into
the five-cup measure and
then refill the three-cup
measure with three more
cups of flour. When he
adds this to the five-cup
measure, he'll have a total
of four cups. Next stop,
delicious cookies!

109. Green. The hints are in the
words "initially" and "the
color": **G**rows **R**yegrass
Everywhere **E**lk **N**eed =
green.

110. H for Happy. These are
the seven dwarfs from
Disney's *Snow White and
the Seven Dwarfs*: Grumpy,
Sleepy, Bashful.

111. Hang up/hang out.

112. Chaimaa buys a book of
matches and a candle.
Once lit, the candle can fill
a room with light.

113. A needle. The hole where
the thread goes through a
needle is called an "eye."

114. Light the end of one rope
and burn it entirely (30
minutes). Then, light
the second rope at both
ends. Since it is burning
from two points, it will
only take 15 minutes for
it to burn entirely—30
minutes plus 15 minutes
equals 45 minutes.

115. Be/Bee/*B*. "Be" means
to exist, but it sounds like
"bee," the insect. If you
remove the "e" or "ee"
from either word, you still
have the first letter, *B*.

116. FB for Frodo Baggins. These are the members of the Fellowship of the Ring from *The Lord of the Rings* by J. R. R. Tolkien: Samwise Gamgee, Meriadoc Brandybuck, Peregrin Took, Gandalf, Legolas, Gimli, Boromir, Aragorn, and Frodo Baggins.

117. Zachary is walking.

118. Portland (Oregon and Maine).

119. The moon. The moon is "no more than a month old" because the lunar cycle lasts one month. On the night of a new moon, the moon is too dark for us to see it.

120. Five pounds.

This puzzle can be expressed in the following equation: $1D + 2D + 3D = 30$, where D is Doorstop's weight (with Shelley weighing twice as much and Scooter weighing three times as much). Since the total can be expressed as $6D = 30$, and 30 divided by 6 equals 5, Doorstop weighs five pounds.

121. A beehive. The "swords" are the bees' stingers. The "gold" is the honey.

122. When you're on Mars.

123. Achraf's own glasses fell off his face and into the sink!

124. A ladder.

125. Ton—Tone—Atone. A "ton" is 2,000 pounds. A "tone" is a single musical note. To "atone" is to make amends for something or to apologize.

126. Q, for Queen. These are chess pieces: King, Queen, Bishop, Knight, Rook, and Pawn.

127. Noon. The clues "last" and "time" hint that you're looking for a time in the last letters of the words. Therefore, oxe**N** g**O** t**O** tow**N** = noon.

128. Three turtles, two birds, and a lizard.

This riddle takes some math (or some trial and error). If we give each animal a letter (T, B, and L), we know that Jacinta's pets total T + B + L. Now we can look at each statement individually. "I have all turtles except three." This means that everything but turtles equals 3, which can be written as B + L = 3. Likewise, T + L = 4 (all birds except four) and T + B = 5 (all lizards except five). Then we can add these equations together to see how many total animals Jacinta has (except for cats, of course). Because T, B, and L all occur two times on the left side of the equation, and the total of all the numbers on the right side of the equation is 12, we can write it out as 2(T + B + L) = 12. Now, all we have to do is divide the right side by 2 to discover that Jacinta has six pets that are not cats. If we apply this to the original statements, we learn that she has three turtles, two birds, and a lizard.

129. The letter *D*.

130. Your reflection.

131. Food.

132. Six.

133. A chair!

134. Downpour.

135. She picks up the second glass and pours the juice into the fifth glass. Now, she has full-empty-full-empty-full-empty.

136. Tamara doesn't want to forget her lunch, so she puts one of her shoes in front of the refrigerator as a reminder. Before she leaves to catch the bus, she grabs her lunch out of the fridge and puts on her second shoe.

137. SA for South America. These are the seven continents: Africa, Australia, Europe, Asia, Antarctica, North

America, and South America.

138. A sea lion!

139. Marie wrote the instructions when she was a child. Now her legs are longer and her steps are bigger.

140. A kite. Kites have a stabilizing part called a "tail" in addition to the string you hold.

141. A lighthouse.

142. Four. No matter what color socks you pull out, if you pull out four, you'll have at least two of the same color.

143. Only once. After that, you will be subtracting 2 from 28, etc.

144. Try on/try out.

145. He kept hitting fowl (foul) balls!

146. Your teeth! No two people have exactly the same pattern of teeth.

147. A tree. You can find out how many years a tree has been alive by counting the rings in a crosscut of its trunk, with each ring representing one year.

148. There are several ways to accomplish this, but here's the easiest: Before Karim starts baking, he should flip both timers. When the 7-minute timer finishes, he should stop the 11-minute timer (turning it on its side so that the sand doesn't keep going). He'll have 4 minutes of sand in this timer. At this point, he should put the cookies in the oven. Then, he can start the remaining 4 minutes. When those finish, he can flip the 11-minute timer again. $11 + 4 = 15$.

149. Say the "magic word" (please)—it just might work!

150. A baseball team.

151. *T*. A "tee" is what you put a golf ball on before hitting it.

152. The BULLdozer.

153. Fluffy is a cat.

154. R for Re. These are the first letters of the solfège sounds for teaching the scale: Do Re Mi Fa So La Ti Do.

155. Thurs(day). The clues here are "in the middle" and "day," so you're looking for a day from the letters in the middle of these words: pe**T**er, was**H**ed, yo**U**r, shi**R**ts, du**S**tin.

156. You can add "end" after them to get a new word.

157. A shadow.

158. A pen.

159. ND, as in "first," "second," "third," etc.

160. Time!

161. Frankie visited five foreign embassies with locations in Honolulu. Every embassy is considered the property of its home country, even if it's in the middle of an American city.

162. N for Nickel. These are coins in order of value: penny, nickel, dime, quarter, half dollar.

163. Throw away/throw up.

164. Fortnight. A "fortnight" is another word for two weeks, shortened from "fourteen nights." Fortnite is a popular computer game.

165. G for Gretel. From the fairy tale, "Hansel and Gretel."

166. Silence.

167. Dogs. The first part ("at last") shows you where to find the "animals": coul**D** pedr**O** brin**G** hi**S** = dogs.

168. An hourglass.

169. O, N, and D for October, November, and December.

170. A penny.

171. One is bad money and one is a mad bunny!

172. Crayons. Crayons melt when you heat them.

173. A cupcake!

174. He had a magic carpet!

175. A bat. (The animal or the piece of sports equipment.)

Matchstick Puzzles

1.

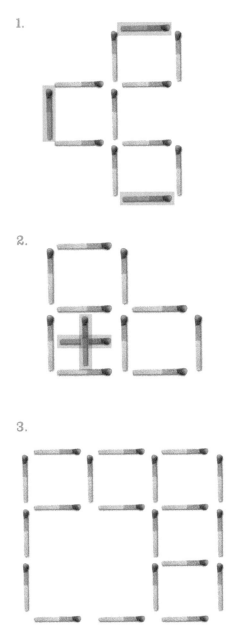

2.

3.

DANIELLE HALL has loved puzzles from an early age and enjoyed old computer games like *The 7th Guest* and *Myst*. She has 10 years of teaching experience, including in North Carolina, Puerto Rico, and Germany. Currently, she makes digital escape games for middle- and high-schoolers. Danielle loves reading, running, and swing dancing. One day, she hopes to visit Machu Picchu. She lives with her wife and pets, Padfoot and Crookshanks, in Astoria, Oregon. Visit her at teachnouvelle.com.

MARY KATE MCDEVITT is an illustrator and letterer working and living in Philadelphia, PA. Her work has appeared in numerous publications, including *The New York Times, The Washington Post,* and *O Magazine*. She has worked with such clients as Target, Pixar, Fox Broadcasting, and Adobe. When Mary Kate is not in the studio, she hosts workshops on lettering and illustration. In her free time, she can be found exploring the historic streets of Philadelphia, working on house projects, in the garden, or hanging out with her cats, Peppy Mew Mew and GC, and her old dog, Fritz.